CHANGE

FROM THE

INSIDE OUT

MAKING YOU, YOUR TEAM,
AND YOUR ORGANIZATION
CHANGE-CAPABLE

CHANGE

FROM THE

INSIDE OUT

ERIKA ANDERSEN

BK
Berrett–Koehler Publishers, Inc.

Berrett-Koehler Publishers, Inc.
1333 Broadway, Suite 1000
Oakland, CA 94612-1921
Tel: (510) 817-2277
Fax: (510) 817-2278
www.bkconnection.com

ORDERING INFORMATION

Quantity sales. Special discounts are available on quantity purchases by corporations, associations, and others. For details, contact the "Special Sales Department" at the Berrett-Koehler address above.
Individual sales. Berrett-Koehler publications are available through most bookstores. They can also be ordered directly from Berrett-Koehler: Tel: (800) 929-2929; Fax: (802) 864-7626; www.bkconnection.com.
Orders for college textbook/course adoption use. Please contact Berrett-Koehler:
Tel: (800) 929-2929; Fax: (802) 864-7626.

Distributed to the US trade and internationally by Penguin Random House Publisher Services.
Berrett-Koehler and the BK logo are registered trademarks of Berrett-Koehler Publishers, Inc.

Printed in Canada

Berrett-Koehler books are printed on long-lasting acid-free paper. When it is available, we choose paper that has been manufactured by environmentally responsible processes. These may include using trees grown in sustainable forests, incorporating recycled paper, minimizing chlorine in bleaching, or recycling the energy produced at the paper mill.

Library of Congress Cataloging-in-Publication Data

Names: Andersen, Erika, author.
    Title: Change from the inside out : making you, your team, and your organization change-capable / Erika Andersen.
    Description: First edition. | Oakland, CA : Berrett-Koehler Publishers, Inc., [2021] | Includes bibliographical references and index. | Summary: "Change initiatives fail because humans are hard-wired to return to what's worked for them in the past. This book offers a straightforward process for building support for change from the ground up" —Provided by publisher.
    Identifiers: LCCN 2021020324 | ISBN 9781523000395 (hardcover) | ISBN 9781523000401 (adobe pdf) | ISBN 9781523000418 (epub)
    Subjects: LCSH: Organizational change. | Teams in the workplace. | Leadership.
    Classification: LCC HD58.8 .A679 2021 | DDC 658.4/06—dc23
    LC record available at https://lccn.loc.gov/2021020324

FIRST EDITION

29 28 27 26 25 24 23 22 21 | 10 9 8 7 6 5 4 3 2 1

Book design and producton: BookMatters; copyediting: Amy Smith Bell; proofing: Janet Reed Blake; indexing: Leonard Rosenbaum; graphic design: Susan Malikowski, DesignLeaf Studio; cover design: Rob Johnson, Toprotype Inc.

My small flock—heart, mind, body, soul—rises together, wheels away
On a touch, a laugh;
Heads unerringly to that warmest place,
Us.

CONTENTS

Preface   ix

ONE How Change Has Changed   1

TWO We Prefer Stability   10

THREE Let the Rewiring Begin   15

FOUR Changing on Three Levels   34
Leaders, Individuals, and Organizations

FIVE The Five-Step Change Model   66

SIX Start at the Beginning   88
STEP 1 *Clarify the Change and Why It's Needed*

SEVEN What Change Will Bring   118
STEP 2 *Envision the Future State*

EIGHT The Heart of the Effort   134
STEP 3 *Build the Change*

NINE Engaging the Whole Organization   175

STEP 4 *Lead the Transition*

TEN To the Future   206

STEP 5 *Keep the Change Going*

ELEVEN On Becoming Change-Capable   224

Notes   229

Acknowledgments   235

Index   237

About the Author   247

About Proteus   249

PREFACE

First, Why You Need This Book

Unless you've been living on another planet, the past few years have shown that we're in a time of unimagined, unrelenting, and ever-increasing change. And we're not very good at it. This book can help.

For more than thirty years, my colleagues and I at Proteus have been helping people clarify and move toward their hoped-for future. Over the past decade we've focused especially on supporting clients through the individual and organizational changes they need to make in order to achieve those envisioned futures. In doing this work, we discovered something simple, predictable, and powerful: the mindset-based shift that each of us must go through in order to make any change.

Throughout this book I'll share that process with you: what that mindset shift is, how it works, and what gets in the way of making it. More important, I'll explain practically how to make that shift faster, easier, and less painful. We'll focus on how you can make that mindset shift for yourself; how you can support those you lead to make that shift; and finally how you can catalyze and cascade that shift throughout your whole organization. That's good news for you as a leader and for everyone in your organization. You'll be able to use the understanding, tools, and approaches outlined throughout this book to guide your people through change in a way that builds their understanding and buy-in and supports their success. At the same time you'll be able to focus clearly on the nuts-and-bolts steps necessary to execute any major transformation—making organizational change less disruptive and more beneficial for your employees and your business as well as for those who look to your business for products and services.

In other words, this book can help you, your people, and your organization become more change-capable—better able to make the changes facing you now and to continue making the necessary changes in response to our ever-changing world. Let's get started.

ONE

How Change Has Changed

We got our first TV when my little brother was a baby. I don't remember how it got into our sunroom—whether my parents picked it up at the store or someone delivered it. But one day it was just there, this beautiful shiny wooden console with the little rectangular glass screen. My mom turned the knob to "on," adjusted the volume, and sat down with the baby. We three older kids sat on the floor, clustered around her feet. And suddenly there was sound and movement: a cartoon. My mother settled back with a sigh, Kurt asleep on her lap, and Kristi and David and I stared, mesmerized.

I don't remember being particularly astonished—I was only three, so everything in my life was new and interesting. I had no reference point for understanding what a huge change this was from everything pre-TV: the whole world brought into our house in this new and living way. My parents got it, though. I vaguely remember pieces of conversations, partly excited and partly proud, about the big changes in the world. It seemed to them that everything had sped up after The War (their name for World War II, always with initial caps implied). TV and antibiotics and everyday air travel—the future for sure, with new things happening all the time.

Yet, compared to today, the changes of sixty years ago were almost stately in their unfolding. We generally had time, back then, to get our minds and our habits completely adjusted to a change before it changed again. For instance, by the time most people in the United States, my folks included, acquired the next version of television technology—a color TV to replace the old black-and-white—we had all had almost a decade to incorporate television into our daily lives. And incorporate it we certainly had. It was our second stop after coming home from school: into the kitchen to scrounge a snack and say hi to Mom, then to the playroom to switch on the TV and watch Loony Tunes before doing our homework. Sunday nights, the whole family would eat popcorn and watch *Bonanza*, *Gunsmoke*, and *The Ed Sullivan Show*. In other words, we were completely ready for this next iteration of TV when it arrived. Being able to watch our favorite programs "in living color," as the ads promised, was a cool though not shocking advance. The red, blue, green, and yellow fireworks at the beginning of Walt Disney's *Wonderful World of Color* were a delight, not a disruption.

In the middle of the twentieth century, this was the pace of most change. Things pretty much stayed the same, day-to-day and year-to-year; when they changed, they changed gradually. My dad and my friends' dads mostly continued working at the same jobs, with the same companies; most of our moms stayed home and took care of us and the household, and perhaps did volunteer or community work. I went to the same high school my older siblings had attended, which my younger brother would attend after me. It may have seemed like a modern, fast-changing world to my parents, but big changes like the advent of TV were still far enough apart to feel like spice in a well-known dish. The world was a fairly stable place. We had a set of World Book encyclopedias—the mid-twentieth-century version of the Internet—and every year the World Book company would send us an update for the previous year. All the important changes and discoveries for 1959 or 1962 fit easily into one slim volume.

Then, in the late 1960s, change started to accelerate—both culturally and technologically. President Kennedy had declared that we should put a man on the moon by the end of the decade, and we did. Many more women began to seek higher education and to enter the workforce, and common assumptions about gender roles began to be questioned. People of color began to ask—and then demand—that they be treated as full and equal citizens. Computers, which had been room-sized behemoths programmed by specially trained professionals using punch cards, shrank to suitcase size, then even smaller. The first "personal computers," meant to be used by individuals, even at home, went on sale in the mid-1970s. By the mid-1980s, about one in ten households had personal computers; by the mid-1990s, that number had grown to three in ten. And that was only the beginning.

Today we all wear computers on our wrists or keep them in our pockets and purses, computers hundreds of times faster and more powerful than their predecessors of a few decades ago. Their capabilities and design evolve continuously—every few months bringing technological change as significant as the change from black-and-white to color TV. The United States has had a Black president, and the US vice president is a woman of color; women and people of color lead countries, companies, and communities all over the world. Global connection to social media ensures that any major event (and too many minor ones) are communicated around the world in hours or minutes. The pace of change in organizations has accelerated and is accelerating in the same way. Here's a glimpse into just two of these shifts, from a report on changes in the American workplace by Pew Research: "A key factor [in this change] is the decline in manufacturing employment, by about a third just since 1990. Meanwhile, employment in knowledge-intensive and service-oriented sectors, such as education, health, and professional and business services, has about doubled. Underlying factors such as globalization, outsourcing of jobs and technological change are among the key forces contributing to the transformation."[1]

Think about that for just a minute. Even though the Pew report conveys this information dispassionately (no exclamation points or italics), this is huge. Over the past thirty years one-third of US manufacturing jobs—the mainstay of American advancement and job creation since the beginning of the twentieth century—have disappeared, gone the way of the dinosaur. Over the same time period, the demand for knowledge- and service-based jobs has doubled. In response to these shifts, thousands of companies that didn't exist thirty years ago have come into existence, and in some cases grown exponentially (think Apple, Google, and Amazon). Thousands more have withered and died or dramatically transformed (think Barnes & Noble, any car company, and the entire music industry).

As an employee in an organization, all of this combines to feel like near-continuous change. A few decades ago, being part of an organizational redesign was a fairly uncommon phenomenon that we as employees had to suffer through: our organization would, in effect, get picked up, shaken, and set back down again, and—*whew*—that was it for a while. Now, there are changes big and small happening to us and around us on an almost daily basis: changes in who we report to, how our work gets done, what our jobs entail, and—more fundamentally—changes in who owns our company, what our mission is, what are the services or products we produce, who the customer is and what they expect from us. Consider, for instance, cable installers. Until about fifteen years ago, cable providers in the United States had almost no competition. If your house was in, say, the Comcast "footprint," Comcast was your only choice if you wanted cable television. Satellite companies like Dish and DIRECTV had fairly small subscriber bases in the early 2000s and weren't yet seen by the cable companies as a big threat. Therefore cable providers didn't have to worry too much about delivering great customer service, and the installer's job was straightforward: go into your house and connect the fiber optic cable to your new set-top box, and the box to your TV set. The end.

Then the satellite companies started to grow in reach and influence, and the telcos (a word coined in the mid-1970s and popularized by the mid-1990s as a conflation of "telephone" and "companies") were getting into the picture as distributors of video content as well. Suddenly the cable operators had real competition and had to completely rethink their approach to customers. At the same time, the technology behind the TV-watching experience was also changing dramatically. The DVR (digital video recorder) debuted in 1999, with the launch of TiVo and ReplayTV. This seemed like a true herald of twenty-first-century tech: being able to set up your DVR to record shows so you could watch them later at your leisure, even fast-forwarding through commercials, pausing while you went to get a snack, or instantly rewatching the good parts. But the technology kept evolving: DVRs were incorporated into cable and satellite set-top boxes and then into TVs. Soon, cable and satellite operators created VOD (video on demand), so consumers could watch shows whenever they wanted. Streaming services—like Netflix, Amazon Prime, and Hulu—offered yet another option for anytime viewing as well as their own high-quality original content. Most recently, streaming players like Roku put all the options in one place. With so many new choices for taking in video content, many consumers—especially those in their twenties and thirties—are opting out of cable altogether. It's estimated that forty-eight million US households have either dropped their pay TV subscriptions or have decided never to sign up in the first place.[2]

Today, operating in this continually changing environment, that beleaguered cable installer who fifteen or twenty years ago only had to worry about getting your box installed correctly is now the main connection point between the cable company and you, the consumer. Not only does she or he have to be the helpful and positive personal representative of the cable company to its customers (because good customer service becomes a key business driver when there are competitors for that customer), the installer also has to be both knowledgeable and articulate about all the new options available to you as a cable customer—not just your cable subscription but also broadband, VOIP phone, wireless provision, and even home security. "And, oh by the way," asks the customer (who is also at the mercy of all these changes) of the cable installer, "how does my Smart TV work with all these choices?"

Behind that cable installer, these changes ripple through every single one of the thousands of employees in the cable company: each service person at a call center who is expected to have more knowledge and a higher level of customer service capability while using new work processes; every marketer who is figuring out how to communicate these ever-evolving products and services; every product developer who is tasked with keeping up with both the consumer's expectations and the competition; every leader who is trying to stay on top of all these changes while inspiring and directing an ever-changing workforce. Because organizations are so complex and our lives are so interconnected by technology and communication, every substantive change in how we do business can affect millions of people—and the possibility of unintended consequence rises exponentially with every change.

Whew.

This degree of change isn't happening in just a few obvious industries like media or technology. A few years ago, I spoke to the annual convention of the global nonprofit Special Libraries Association, for professionals who work in and manage libraries of information specific to industries or knowledge areas. I made this same point about change—its magnitude and constancy in every area of our lives—and I asked everyone whose job *had not changed at all* in the preceding twelve months to raise his or her hand. Of the thousand or so people in the audience, maybe thirty put their hands in the air.

So, here we all are. Change—rapid, fundamental, and continuous—affects every aspect of our lives. Why am I telling you this? When I started my company in 1990, we named it Proteus, after the shape-shifting Greek sea-god whose mythology said that if you could find and hold on to him, no matter what form he assumed, he would be forced to reveal the future to you. We saw even then that the world was speeding up and changing dramatically, and that those shifts would call for new ways of responding. Understanding this, we defined our mission in this way: We help clients clarify and move toward their hoped-for future. Ever since, we've offered our services with that mission in mind; we've worked with clients to help them craft a clear vision of the future they want to create for themselves and to build the skills and knowledge necessary to move in that direction. However, over the past decade we've seen that an ever larger part of helping our clients move toward their hoped-for future now involves helping them with change itself. This involves supporting our clients to understand how change works and how we can (and need to) rewire ourselves and our organizations to be able to create a successful future in an era of continuous and ever-expanding change.

That's why I've written this book. I hope to offer you core insights combined with practical new ways of thinking and behaving that will make it easier for you to move through the changes that confront you now. It will also provide tools you can use to help those around you navigate change as well. These models, skills, and mindset will serve you not just with today's changes but in moving through all the changes yet to come. I'm not here to give you single-change advice. I'm here to prepare you to be change-capable and even change-positive through your life—to have the tools you need to evolve and thrive at the pace of change…which I have no reason to believe will be slowing down. In fact, all signs point to continued acceleration.[3]

One last thing: Because we humans love stories—and because stories are such an ageless way to communicate important ideas—I'll tell you a story about change that will travel through the journey of this book with us. I'd like to introduce you to the folks at Moment Jewelry, a family business that finds itself facing the need for major change:

Jade Marandaz sits in the break room on the second floor of the Moment Jewelry building in Stamford, Connecticut, absently stirring her coffee as she stares out the floor-to-ceiling window to the street below. Shoppers and office workers stream in both directions, bundled in coats, hats, and gloves, their breath fogging the air as they rush between errands, lunch, and work. She notices that only a few of them are walking into the Moment store's entrance, directly below where she's sitting.

Her dad, Dan, walks into the break room, pops a coffee pod into the machine, and waits for his cup to fill. He watches Jade watching the people outside. She doesn't seem to notice him. "Hey, Jade," he says finally, bringing his coffee to the table and sitting down next to her. "Your coffee's getting cold."

"Hi, Papa." She glances down at her cup and pushes it away. "Steven showed me the preliminary Black Friday numbers. We don't have Danbury and Waterbury yet." She shakes her head and sighs. "I've got to convince James to get on the same accounting system. But in any case, what we have so far doesn't look great."

"I saw the numbers," Dan responds. "They're not terrible."

"But they're not good—flat to last year, if that. Papa, if you're serious about me becoming CEO next year, you've got to start focusing on this with me. We're not growing."

Dan stands up and closes the break room door. "You know, mija, I am with you. I just don't want to worry anybody."

"Maybe we should worry more." Jade frowns, tapping her stir stick on the table.

"Worry without a solution is just upsetting." Dan leans forward to catch his daughter's eyes. "I know we need to make some changes— I do listen to you. We hired Rajiv as CTO, right?"

"Yes, and he's a big step in the right direction—but there's so much more we need to do. Our systems are a mess, the website isn't much more than a good-looking online billboard, and our store staff are sweet, but they're just order takers, for the most part..."

Dan puts his hand on her arm. "I don't disagree with anything you're saying. But you're talking about a lot of change all at once. When your aunt Ellen and I started Moment, we wanted to grow— and we have grown and improved a lot along the way. But we've done it carefully, and we've built a place where people like to work, a family place—and we have good quality, affordable products. You know we've had some of the same customers, here in Stamford especially, ever since we opened in '88. I agree we need to think about upgrading in some areas, but we don't want to get rid of what's working, and we need to be careful not to stir everything up too much—we don't want to lose people...staff or customers."

Jade turns to him, her expression serious. "Papa, I'm worried if we don't stir everything up, we could fail." As Dan shakes his head, she continues. "I'm not kidding, Papa, and I'm not being dramatic. I know how much you value stability. And it's just not enough anymore. It's not."

TWO

We Prefer Stability

Homeostasis, from the Greek words for "same" and "steady,"
refers to any process that living things use to actively maintain fairly stable conditions necessary for survival.

—*Emeritus professor Kelvin Rodolfo*

Though the word *homeostasis* was coined less than a hundred years ago,
it describes a phenomenon as old as humanity.[4] For as long as we've
been around, homeostasis—a kind of dynamic stability—has been es-
sential to our well-being. For example, if we get too hot, we have bodily
mechanisms like sweating to cool us back to an optimal temperature.
And if those don't work, we've learned to apply external balancers: move
into the shade, find cool water to pour over ourselves and/or drink. If we
get too cold, we put on more covering. Too low on fuel, we get hungry,
and we eat. Humans are programmed to stay within a set of physical
parameters that keep us alive and healthy, and that we experience as
"comfortable."

Historically, sociological homeostasis has also served us well. Being
able to create and maintain stable family groups and larger working
groups—village, farm, or factory—made it more likely that those
groups would be able, over time, to prosper and grow. Doing our work
in the same ways, cultivating and eating the same foods, having the
same expectations of each other that had been shown to work well for

many years, all of this was a good hedge against inevitable external disruption—crop failure, disease, invasion. As soon as the unusual circumstance was past, we learned to go back to "normal" as quickly as possible. In short: throughout the vast majority of human history, significant change was almost invariably a threat to our well-being and needed to be managed or removed immediately in order to return to homeostasis, the status quo.

This may sound like ancient history, but that preference for the status quo is very much with us today. Most modern-day "conservative" political movements, for instance, are primarily in favor of returning to what their adherents see as a healthier, safer homeostasis of the past: societal rules and expectations that "worked well" (at least for some people) for many years, and to which we should, adherents believe, return. As a species and as individuals, we have been programmed for many thousands of years to believe that in order to survive, we have to define "normal" and then stay as close to that definition as we possibly can. This bias toward sameness and stability has in fact always been a powerful restraining influence on change. During the past few hundred years, as advances in communication and technology have been accelerating factors, our deeply wired-in preference for homeostasis has served as a consistent brake on that acceleration.

For example, in the mid-seventeenth century, scientists began to be able to see microorganisms under newly developed microscopes and began to posit these tiny creatures as a source of infection and disease. Over the next two hundred years, more and more scientific evidence supported this new "germ theory."[5] In the mid-nineteenth century, a doctor named Ignaz Semmelweis conducted an experiment. He made doctors wash their hands with chlorinated lime water before examining women giving birth. Over one year Semmelweis documented a sudden and dramatic reduction in the mortality rate of women attended in childbirth by these doctors—from 18 percent to 2.2 percent.[6] But it was another fifty years before most doctors were regularly washing their hands between patients. Why? Because it was different from what they'd always done and what they assumed was best; it wasn't "normal." It seems they were uncomfortable accepting this new idea that implied that they—takers of the Hippocratic oath, those most knowledgeable about illnesses and their treatment—were actually making their patients sick, or even killing them.

If this single, seemingly simple change based on an ever-increasing body of data generated ongoing, entrenched negativity or dismissal for hundreds of years, it's no wonder this age of continuous change makes us anxious! At work, for instance, just when we've figured out what's "normal"—how things work, who is important, what the company does and why—it all shifts out from under us. Suddenly we're reporting to someone new, the group next to us has been outsourced, our core work processes have changed, and the department goals have altered dramatically. And then, just as we're starting to figure out this new normal, to accept it as the way things are and take a breath—everything changes again. It's exhausting. It's the way life is now, and it's just going to keep speeding up.

So here we are with this deeply wired-in, ancient drive toward homeostasis. Instead of serving us almost all the time, as it has for millennia, this drive now only serves us some of the time. It serves us physiologically: it's still important to keep our bodies within certain parameters of weight, temperature, and hydration to stay healthy and vital. The drive toward homeostasis often serves us interpersonally, too: it's still healthy and important—maybe more than ever—to create and maintain strong, stable human bonds. But organizationally (and I would argue politically, scientifically, psychologically, and economically), we are going to have to let go of our age-old focus on keeping things the same and instead learn to feel comfortable with and to find a new kind of dynamic stability in a state of ongoing change. In order to survive and thrive today and